Burr Oak, Iowa

William Anderson

2023

Carrie, Mary and Laura, a few years after they lived in Burr Oak

The
IOWA STORY
Laura Ingalls Wilder's life in Burr Oak, Iowa

By William Anderson

*Cover art is by distinguished author-illustrator
Cheryl Harness. Many authors credit Laura Ingalls Wilder
as a childhood inspiration, unlocking a love for words and
history. Cheryl is among that group.*

DEDICATION

in appreciation to all of the many volunteers who helped to establish a museum of the childhood home of Laura Ingalls Wilder in the community of Burr Oak, Iowa, and with gratitude to those who have given their time to continuing this piece of "Little House" history.

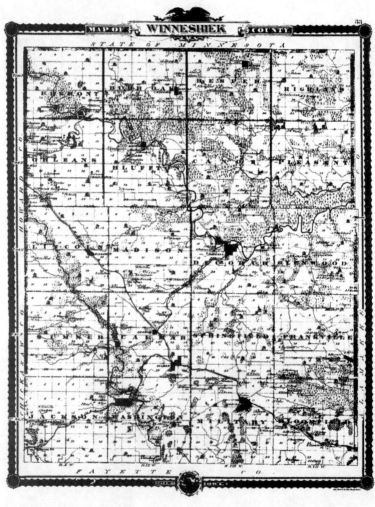

Winneshiek County, Iowa, where two famous American authors lived as children: Laura Ingalls Wilder and Hamlin Garland.

INTRODUCTION

L aura Ingalls Wilder's "Little House" books are perhaps the greatest literary achievements of their kind written in the twentieth century. Although great and widespread popularity and warm affection sometimes detracts from an acceptance of the worth of literature, there is little doubt that the Wilder books are and will remain highly valuable accounts of pioneering in the last great phase of American frontier settlement.

In the "Little House" books, all of the elements of the pioneering experience are carefully drawn. The appeal and lure of the West is evident. The sturdy independence and survival skills necessary in a harsh environment are described. The importance of the small frontier settlements in the economy and social lives of the early settler is conveyed. Because she had lived the life of a pioneer girl, Laura Ingalls Wilder expressed that existence in an effortless but meaningful prose style. Lurking under the simplicity of her writing is the essence of an era.

Laura's eight-volume novel, as she called it, centered around the theme of going west. But during one childhood interlude, her family took, as author Hamlin Garland termed it "the back trail." Garland, whose journeys from Wisconsin to South Dakota roughly paralleled Laura's, wrote of a relentlessly draining western experience, and he abhorred the difficulties of homesteading so much that his goal was to re-establish his parents in Wisconsin, where they had started. He saw no shame in admitting that South Dakota prairie life exacted too great a price for what it returned.

One of Hamlin Garland's first stops on his family's exodus west from Wisconsin was in the northeastern corner of Iowa, in the county of Winneshiek, near Burr Oak. It was in this same vicinity that Laura Ingalls Wilder once lived, when her family "back-trailed" from harsh conditions in western Minnesota.

Laura did not write for publication about her family's year in Burr Oak. She did not choose to interrupt her "going west" saga. But today, her life is so synonymous with the pioneering and west-moving experience, that no aspect of it is being overlooked by her readers. What occurred with the Ingalls family in Burr Oak seems as significant as what they encountered in Pepin, Wisconsin or Walnut Grove, Minnesota or DeSmet, South Dakota.

As a child, on my first visit to the Laura Ingalls Wilder Home and Museum in Mansfield, Missouri, I first learned that there had been an interlude in the "Little House" book sequence which had taken the Ingalls family to Iowa. The first curators, Mr. and Mrs. L.D. Lichty, told me sketchily about the Burr Oak period. My reactions were both surprise that Laura had not written ALL the truth, and curiosity as to what life had been like for the Ingallses during their Iowa year.

Since then, many of those questions have been answered. New and dramatic material has come to light, facts and details have been pieced together to re-create the missing year. From this information, a museum dedicated to the Ingalls history in Burr Oak has emerged. And Burr Oak itself has taken its place as one of the "little towns" now a literary landmark because Laura Ingalls Wilder once lived there.

While I have written about Burr Oak many times in other books and articles, and have visited the site several times, this is the first occasion I have had to piece all the available data together and to record under one cover the story of the missing year.

The urging of the Laura Ingalls Wilder Park and Museum Board in Burr Oak, Iowa has resulted in this project. Valuable assistance in compiling the facts and gathering impressions of Burr Oak have come from David De Cou and Lorraine Houck, who have served on both the restoration project and the board of the historic Masters Hotel, home of the Ingalls family. Evelyn Underbakke, the long-time director of the museum and its tours, has been a solid source of information, and most importantly, the prodding force in getting the research and writing completed.

Laura Ingalls Wilder once called her books "stories that had to be told." She said that her childhood had been "altogether too important to be lost." Her experiences in Burr Oak were part of that pioneer life. They, too, are "too important to be lost."

W.T.A.
March 1990

I. BURR OAK: THE MISSING ERA OF LAURA'S BOOKS

When readers of Laura Ingalls Wilder's "Little House" series complete the last chapter of *On the Banks of Plum Creek*, a satisfied feeling of contentment is evident. The grasshopper plague had been weathered, the farm along Plum Creek, near Walnut Grove, Minnesota had been established, and good times seemed to be ahead. There was hope and security in Pa's voice when he says, in the last lines of *Plum Creek*, "Look, Caroline, how Laura's eyes are shining."

When the next book in the series, *By the Shores of Silver Lake* opens, there is only a hint of what years 1875 through 1879 have brought to Charles and Caroline Ingalls and their daughters. Laura tells that Grace, the youngest child, has been born, but not that a baby son had been born and died. Readers learn that Mary Ingalls lost her eyesight, but not that the origin of the illness can be traced back several years before she became blind in 1879. And most significantly omitted from Laura's quick exposition in *Silver Lake* is the fact that the Ingalls family traveled east from Walnut Grove during the period between the two books. For more than a year, they lived in the northeastern corner of Iowa, at the town of Burr Oak.

The reasons for Laura's omission of Burr Oak, Iowa from her series of books are many. Most obviously, that era in her family life was a discouraging one, with many difficulties and disappointments. Her series of books had as its theme the concept of moving west, and the Burr Oak era dealt with back-tracking. For Pa Ingalls, the move to Iowa was a loss of the independent pioneering aspect of forging westward.

More complex was the literary necessity of deleting several years of Laura's chronological age from the story line of the "Little House" books. Laura had no idea, when she wrote *Little House in the Big Woods*, that she was commencing a series of books which readers would follow carefully from one volume to another, with full attention to dates, time and details all coinciding with the previous story. When she completed *On the Banks of Plum Creek*, she needed to account for two years she had earlier added to Laura's age. Rose Wilder Lane told this author why. . .*

It may interest you to know why Burr Oak, Iowa was left

---

* Letter from Rose Wilder Lane to William Anderson, June 17, 1966.

1

*out of the books. My mother was three years old in **Little House in the Big Woods.** She wrote about her birthday, when--as was customary--she was given three spanks (by Pa) and "one to grow on". Harper Brothers (then her publisher; the name now changed to Harper and Row) would not print this; the editors insisted that no child has a memory before the age of five. (This is absurd, of course; it is a belief of professional psychologists; I myself recall events in my second year--before I was two years old, and so do many other persons.) There was a long wrangle about this but Harpers refused to publish the book without the change, and finally my mother agreed to be five years old in the book. This would make her two years older than she really was, through all the other books. So she left out the two years spent in Burr Oak, partly to make her age correct and partly because Burr Oak was not too different from the **Little Town** (DeSmet) that she wrote about later. Though Burr Oak was then an old town, built of red brick and **feeling** old. . .*

In the same vein, Rose Wilder Lane wrote to Irene V. Lichty, first curator of the Laura Ingalls Wilder Home and Museum in Mansfield, Missouri, who was constantly asked to explain the time which elapsed in Burr Oak. Rose explained:

My mother could not possibly have written about everything that happened even in her "growing up" years. . .All that my mother wrote was truth although she could not write everything that happened in her childhood.

Other than in personal letters to Rose, the only other place in which Laura Ingalls Wilder wrote extensively about life in Burr Oak was in her first book-length manuscript, *Pioneer Girl.* When her urge to write about her life finally found its way to paper, Laura wrote the first-person autobiography recounting her life from age three to eighteen. She completed the account in 1930, and with the help of Rose's literary agent, it was circulated among several New York publishing houses. When it failed to find an interested publisher, Laura re-worked her material and produced *Little House in the Big Woods.*

The absence of stories about Laura's life in Burr Oak in her published books seems to be best explained in her own words about the truth and accuracy of what she wrote. "I lived everything told of in the 'Little House' books," she said, "but I did not write *all* the truth."

The rest of the story, the untold year the Ingalls family spent in Burr Oak, Iowa, can fortunately be told here.

2

Laura Ingalls Wilder

*Illustration from **Little House on the Prairie** by Helen Sewell.*
©1935 by Harper and Brothers.

II. REFUGEES FROM GRASSHOPPER COUNTRY

The Ingalls family were pioneers, as Laura said, "to a marked degree". They were among the great influx of Americans, who, after the Civil War, joined the westward movement. In that last era of pioneering, Laura had the unique opportunity to experience the slow movement of a white-topped prairie schooner inching across unsettled lands. In her girlhood was the hardship and achievement of watching homesteads become established, helping new towns being built and seeing civilization replace the untamed western prairies.

For Laura, her first memories of life began in the woods near Pepin, Wisconsin, where her parents settled after their 1860 marriage. There Mary was born in 1865 and Laura in 1867. From there, in 1869, the family moved to Indian Territory in southern Kansas. While there, in 1870, Carrie, the third daughter was born. But Pa Ingalls' dream of a prairie homestead was interrupted by the fact that technically the land he chose was still Osage Indian reservation country. In 1871, Pa and Ma returned to the home they had started from in Pepin.

Their move across Minnesota to the banks of Plum Creek near Walnut Grove, Minnesota in 1873 resumed Pa's search for a home in the west. *On the Banks of Plum Creek* tells of the

4

family's life while building up a home and a farm. It also related, from Laura's girlhood memories, the tragedy of the infamous grasshopper plagues of the mid-1870's. Those discouraging years, when hordes of ravenous grasshoppers devoured crops and grass and "any green thing", wreaked havoc on the Minnesota pioneers. A state-wide problem far more widespread than Laura relates in her book was the serious result.

During the worst of the grasshopper years in 1874, it was estimated that damage to crop production in affected states was $56 million. The misery felt by Laura's family when their crops were destroyed was shared by thousands of farm families like them all over the mid-west. Never again has a plague of grasshoppers been so widespread.

A plague is the best term to describe the onset of the destructive insects. First came the ominous cloud of 'hoppers which could darken the sun and drop to the ground like attacking hordes. Their subsequent munching and eating of crops, gardens, leafing trees and grass left desolate prairies which had seemed so fruitful and flowerful only a short time before.

In Redwood County, where the Ingalls family lived, severe damage was recorded; throughout 28 other Minnesota counties crops were also devastated.

Many of the settlers in southwestern Minnesota left the country following the grasshopper infestation. Others could not afford to leave, or were determined to hang on in hopes of better farming conditions. The Ingalls family reached a compromise. Pa left Ma and the girls on the Plum Creek farm to manage while he walked to the eastern side of the state to work as a harvest hand where the wheat-fields were unaffected by the plague. Most likely Pa worked in Wabasha or Olmstead counties.

The widespread misery caused by the crop failures became a local and state-wide emergency in Minnesota. Newly-formed counties were hard-pressed to meet needs of poverty-stricken residents because they were experiencing little tax revenue from the indigent land-owners. The State of Minnesota eventually set up a relief program to help desperate and near-starving farmers. Applicants for relief were compelled to sign a "pauper's oath", witnessed by four others. After this humiliating oath was signed, the needy person received about two dollars worth of goods, including pork, matches, baking soda and molasses.

The Ingalls family, with their strict code of avoiding any "beholdeness", managed to survive with Pa's earnings in the wheat-fields of eastern Minnesota. But as the crisis situation continued, and the grasshoppers laid eggs for another season of feasting, Pa could see that his dream of a productive western farm was impossible.

When he returned from the harvest season of 1875, Pa and Ma moved Mary, Laura and Carrie to a rented house in Walnut Grove. There, on November 1, 1875, a baby son was born. Pa and Ma's only boy was named Charles Frederick, for Pa, and for Ma's kind stepfather, Frederick Holbrook. The family called him Freddie and they were proud of the little brother.

When the 1876 crops were again affected by the grasshoppers, Pa declared that he had had enough of the "blasted country". In July of 1876, Pa sold the Plum Creek farm to a couple named Keller. Although he would prefer moving west, Pa was persuaded by the Steadmans, who were friends from Walnut Grove, to travel east and settle in Burr Oak, Iowa. William and Maggie Steadman were buying a hotel in Burr Oak, and wanted Pa and Ma to be their partners.

Peter and Eliza Ingalls. (Peter was Pa's brother; Eliza was Ma's sister.)

A letter from Uncle Peter and Aunt Eliza Ingalls assured Pa that he could work in the harvest fields for wages until he was needed in Burr Oak in the autumn. Peter and Eliza urged Pa and Ma to come to their home along the Zumbro River in eastern Minnesota to stay for the summer. So the Ingalls family again packed the covered wagon for the long drive east. "How I wished we were going west!" Laura recalled. "Pa did not like to turn his back on the west either; this I knew, though he didn't say so."

When they settled in with Peter and Eliza, the two families totaled thirteen people. Mary and Laura were glad to become re-acquainted with their cousins, Peter, Alice, Ella, Edith and Lansford. Together, through the late summer and early fall, the cousins worked and played together. To them it was a happy time, but to the adults, there were worries about crops and debts and feeding and clothing and educating all of the cousins. Pa and Ma wondered what luck they would have in Burr Oak. All of their families were concerned that Charles and Caroline could not find a permanent home.

Ma's mother, Charlotte Holbrook, expressed the concern when she wrote her daughter Martha Carpenter: "Did you see Caroline while she was at Peter's? I wonder when they will get too a stopping place. I shall be glad for their sake, they have had a hard time of it since they left Pepin. ...Almost everyone we meet is crying hard times if they lived where the Grasshoppers are..."*

While they were at Peter and Eliza's, Pa and Ma were concerned about their little Freddie's health. The infant was weak and sickly, and though a doctor came, he continued to waste away. On August 27, 1876, Charles Frederick Ingalls died. Laura remembered that "he straightened out his little body and was dead."

They buried Freddie near Uncle Peter's house in the South Troy neighborhood, knowing that soon he would be left alone when the family moved on to Burr Oak. It was a grief Pa and Ma never forgot. Nearly forty years after Freddie's death, Ma mourned him, telling relatives how different everything would be "if Freddie had lived."

Late in the fall, the Ingalls family packed their wagon again, said good-by to the Peter Ingalls family and turned south on the road to Burr Oak, Iowa. They were chilly on the long cold trip, and sad, thinking of the lost brother. They crossed the Minnesota state line and traveled three miles into Iowa, arriving at the village of Burr Oak. As they drove down the long Main Street in search of the Masters Hotel, Pa, Ma, Mary, Laura and Carrie peered anxiously at the town that would be their new home.

*Letter of December 24, 1876, from Rome, Wisconsin.

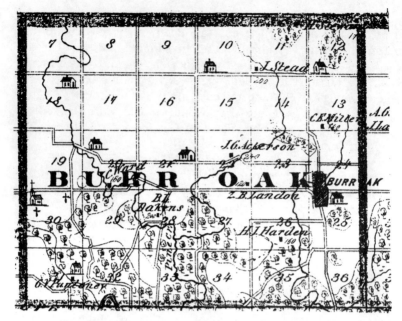

A nineteenth century map of Burr Oak Township

III. Life in Burr Oak and
the Masters Hotel

Burr Oak, in Winneshiek County, Iowa,* was an old town when the Ingalls arrived there to live in the fall of 1876. It was well-established and unlike the new frontier village of Walnut Grove. It was twelve miles north of the busy city of Decorah, the county seat. In its heyday, Burr Oak was a crossroads of the western movement. The road going north led into Minnesota. The trail from the banks of the Mississippi River ran westward through Burr Oak and on through Iowa, Nebraska and points west.

Byron Blackmarr, an early Burr Oak settler, recalled those active, busy Burr Oak years, soon after he arrived there to live in the 1850's. He used to count the pioneer wagons which stopped for the night in Burr Oak, or passed through on the way west. The average each day was 200; sometimes there were as many as 300. At night the houses and yards of Burr Oak would be full of travelers camping. The stock being driven along the wagons created a considerable population in itself. The sound of the

*The town was named for a large grove of burr oak trees on a hill in the north part of town.

sheep bells and cow bells mingling created loud music all through Burr Oak.

Burr Oak was originally settled in 1850. The town ran along an extended Main Street (called State Street), with Silver Creek crossing it on the north edge of the village and Lansing and Spring Streets running east and west in the south end. Because a brick-works was an early industry, many of the buildings in Burr Oak were built of brick. The first school-house was stone. A large stone quarry was just west of the village.

Burr Oak became a significant little town for the area, with many services for the farmers living in the vicinity. There was a blacksmith shop, a harness shop, a livery stable, a creamery and many necessary businesses. A shoemaker and a doctor practiced their trades. Two churches and a school fulfilled the educational and religious needs of the people. The town had two havens for travelers: The American House hotel and the Burr Oak House, known as the Masters Hotel when the Ingalls family arrived.

Ironically, although Laura did not write a book about Burr Oak, someone else did. George Payne Bent, the son of Reverend George Bent, who started serving the Congregational Church in Burr Oak in 1859, wrote Tales of *Travel and Life and Love* in 1924. Though born in Illinois in 1854, he spent the 1860s in Burr Oak. His warm memories of boyhood there were recorded in 147 pages of his self-published autobiography, in which he recounted many of the people and places which Laura Ingalls undoubtedly knew when she came to live in Burr Oak. His book is an outstanding source of details about Burr Oak.

Like Laura, George Bent became prominent in his field. His George P. Bent Company produced thousands of award-winning pianos and organs, and it made the founder of the firm a wealthy man. Like the familiar Lyon and Healy insignia, George Bent's signature adorned all of his finished pianos and organs.

Fortunately, Bent included a plat of Burr Oak in his book. It shows the town very much as the Ingalls family knew it. The Burr Oak House, shown on the map between Lansing and State Streets, was later the hotel which Pa and Ma helped to operate.

An early visitor to Burr Oak spoke glowingly of the location of the town and the beauty of the nearby countryside. "When I saw its location, the beautiful groves which surrounded it on every side, the undulating country in every direction, the limpid stream of pure and sparkling water, cold and clear, I could not fail to admire the judgement of the men who decided upon the site for the town."

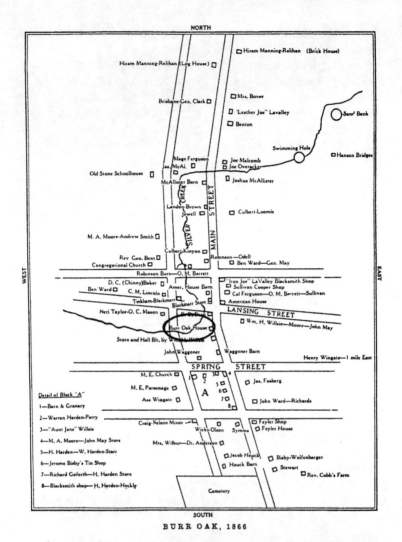

NORTH

Hiram Manning-Relihan (Brick House)

Hiram Manning-Relihan (Log House)

Mrs. Bover

Brisbane-Geo. Clark

"Leather Joe" Lavalley

Sand Bank

Benton

Swimming Hole

Hanson Bridges

Mage Ferguson

Joe Malcomb

Jas. McAl.

Joe Overacker

Old Stone Schoolhouse

McAllister Barn

Joshua McAllister

Landon-Brown

Culbert-Loomis

Jewell

M. A. Moore-Andrew Smith

Culbert-Kinyon

Rev. Geo. Bent

Robinson—Odell

Congregational Church

Ben Ward—Geo. May

Robinson Barn—O. M. Barrett

D. C. (Chinny)Baker

"Iron Joe" LaValley Blacksmith Shop

Ben Ward

C. M. Lincoln

Amer. House Barn

Sullivan Cooper Shop

Cal Ferguson—O. M. Barrett—Sullivan

Tinkham-Blackmarr

Blackmarr Store

American House

Neri Taylor-O. C. Mason

LANSING STREET

Burr Oak House

Wm. H. Willsie—Moore—John May

Store and Hall Blk. by

John Waggoner

Waggoner Barn

Henry Wingate—1 mile East

SPRING STREET

M. E. Church

30

Jas. Fosberg

M. E. Parsonage

Detail of Block "A"

Asa Wingate

John Ward—Richards

A

Craig-Nelson Minor

1—Barn & Granary

Wicks-Olson

Symms

Feyler Shop

Feyler House

2—Warren Harden-Perry

Mrs. Wilbur—Dr. Anderson

3—"Aunt Jane" Willsie

4—M. A. Moore—John May Store

Jacob Houck

Bisby-Wolfenbarger

5—H. Harden—W. Harden-Starr

Houck Barn

Stewart

6—Jerome Bisby's Tin Shop

Rev. Cobb's Farm

7—Richard Goforth—H. Harden Store

8—Blacksmith shop—H. Harden-Hecklg.

Cemetery

WEST

EAST

SILVER CREEK

MAIN STREET

SOUTH

BURR OAK, 1866

Plat map of Burr Oak as taken from George Bent's book "Tales of Travel, Life and Love".

When the Ingalls family drove into Burr Oak late in the dreary autumn following Freddie's death, they were welcomed into the warmth of the Masters Hotel, which was called the Burr Oak House.* The hotel was also called a tavern, as was the custom of the time. It did have a bar-room, but a tavern was more often used to describe a place where travelers ate and slept. The Burr

*In 1880, the population of Burr Oak village was 199, so it was probably very close to that number when the Ingalls family was there in 1876-1877. The rival hotel in town, The American House probably did more business than the Masters Hotel, because it was the headquarters for the stage coach line passing through.

10

Oak House was also a community center, where dances and weddings were held. A few people called it home, and were known as "steady boarders."

Burr Oak House was evolved from a log hotel first built in 1851. In 1856, when the hotel was sold, an addition was constructed. The hotel faced Main Street, and was much larger than it appeared from the street. It was built on the edge of a sloping hill, so it extended down the hill, with a lower level providing kitchen facilities, a large dining room, and possibly a sleeping area. The main floor at street level had two entrances: one leading to the hotel parlor and the other to the bar-room. There was a hotel office and a bedroom off the parlor. A steep stairway led to four second-floor sleeping rooms. Some lodgers slept on cots on the landing at the head of the stairs.

Behind the hotel was a barn, a springhouse with a flowing spring, where milk and butter were kept cool. Silver Creek flowed through the yard; it was full of speckled trout. Laura recalled a fishpond in the backyard.

The most recent owner of the hotel when the Ingalls family arrived to live there was William Masters. His brother Samuel* had settled in Walnut Grove, and then William moved there after selling his hotel to the Steadmans on October 21, 1876. The Steadmans paid $2,000 for the property.

Whether Pa and Ma invested money in the hotel operation is not clear. Perhaps they agreed to help with its management in exchange for meals and living space and wages. Laura later said she knew Pa received very little for his services.

"A very fine place" was the way Laura rememberd the Masters Hotel. Since the parlor bedroom was occupied by the hotel's star boarder, Mr. B.L. Bisbee, and the other rooms must have been reserved for paying guests and steady boarders, it is not known exactly where the Ingalls family and the Steadman family slept. The Steadmans had three sons, Johnny, Ruben and Tommy. There was truly "no room in the inn" for the operators; between them, there were four adults and six children. Certainly Ma and Pa could see when they got settled that there would be no privacy for their own family life.

Pa was constantly busy working around the hotel, but occasionally he played his fiddle in the hotel office. Ma was always tired, it seemed, with helping Mrs. Steadman in cleaning, cooking and laundry around the hotel. Mary and Laura made beds,

* Samuel O. Masters was the grandfather of Aubrey Sherwood (1894-1987), the well known Ingalls-Wilder historian of DeSmet, South Dakota.

11

The Masters Hotel as it looked around the time the Ingalls family lived there.

washed dishes, waited on tables, and Mrs. Steadman assigned them the care of her youngest boy, Tommy.

Mary and Laura, and perhaps little Carrie, who was six, started attending the Burr Oak school, which was across the street and up Spring Street from the hotel. The secondary teacher and principal, William Reed, who boarded at the hotel, was only sixteen when he was in charge of Burr Oak's brick school. When winter approached, a group of bullies in their twenties started attending school for the purpose of fighting the teacher and driving him from town.

Before Christmas, the troublesome students were disrupting the whole school. One morning, the ringleader, Mose, approached Mr. Reed, expecting a fight in which he would win. But instead, Mr. Reed tripped Mose, laid him across his knee and started whipping him soundly with a ruler. "We young ones sat still, watching and hardly breathing," Laura recalled.

When Mr. Reed finished with Mose, he and his friends left the school-room permanently, all the town laughing at them. School then proceeded quietly. Laura used a similar incident in *Farmer Boy*.

The Ingalls family attended the Congregational Church in Burr Oak, and at Christmas, a tree and program were scheduled at the school-house. On Christmas Eve, Laura sat among the Burr Oakers who enjoyed a celebration like the one she described in *On the Banks of Plum Creek*.

12

The Burr Oak Advent Church, now restored.

Otherwise, Laura remembered, Christmas 1876 was bleak for her family. Mrs. Steadman forgot to keep her promise to Mary and Laura of rewarding them with a gift in exchange for their care of her Tommy. Pa and Ma were preoccupied. And then, Mary, Laura and Carrie were sick with measles.

"The hotel was a noisy place to be sick in," Laura remembered. And Burr Oak children were sent in to play with the Ingalls girls so they would be exposed to the measles "to get it over with." Ruben Steadman enjoyed disturbing the sick girls, until he was ill himself.

As winter progressed, Pa and Ma were not pleased with their living arrangements in the hotel. People were constantly coming and going. They disapproved of the bar-room. Amy, the hired girl showed them bullet holes in the kitchen door, which indicated what a drunken man had done right in the hotel. Will Masters, son of the previous owners, had chased his wife Nannie through the kitchen door while he was drunk. His shots had left the holes in the door. Amy's beau was not much better. He was called Hairpin, because he was lean and tall, and he spent much time in the saloon next to the hotel.

13

Burr Oak's "other" hotel, The American House.

Finally, Pa and Ma decided to move away from the hotel. "Steadman handled the money," Laura recalled, "and someway beat Pa out of his share. I don't suppose there was much." But before they moved, Laura had to spend hours pleasing the boarder Mr. Bisbee by learning the musical scales. Up and down she sang, "do, re, me, fa, so, la, ti, do."

Laura's singing lessons and her parents' part in running a hotel were over when Pa rented rooms over Kimball's Grocery. They spent the rest of the winter of 1877 living in the quiet, comfortable rooms. Never again did Pa try to run a hotel.

IV. Burr Oak Days

After leaving the hotel, the Ingalls family once more settled into a routine. Pa started a feed-mill, using his team to turn the mill-stone used in grinding wheat and corn. Ma, who was expecting another baby, liked the quiet of the rooms over Kimball's, the grocery store built in 1856. They were still in sight of the hotel, and much to Ma and Pa's dismay, closer than ever to the Burr Oak saloon.

One night the saloon caught fire. Pa joined a bucket brigade, and the fire was stopped, but he admitted that "If that darn saloon could have gone without burning the whole town, I for one wouldn't have carried one drop of water."

Mary and Laura were enjoying the days in the red brick school. For her twelfth birthday, on January 10, 1877, Mary was given the black embossed *Independent Fifth Reader**. In it were many great speeches, stories, poems and essays, suited to be read

INDEPENDENT

FIFTH READER:

CONTAINING

A PRACTICAL TREATISE ON ELOCUTION, ILLUSTRATED
WITH DIAGRAMS; SELECT AND CLASSIFIED
READINGS AND RECITATIONS; WITH
COPIOUS NOTES AND COMPLETE
SUPPLEMENTARY INDEX.

By J. MADISON WATSON,

A. S. BARNES & COMPANY,
NEW YORK, CHICAGO & NEW ORLEANS.

The reader Mary received on her twelfth birthday in Burr Oak

* During *The Long Winter, Independent Fifth Reader* helped entertain the Ingalls family, as the girls recited favorite pieces. In 1949, Laura presented the book to the Detroit Public Library, where it is now preserved in the Rare Book and Gift Room.

aloud. Mr. Reed was an outstanding elocution teacher, and he taught Mary and Laura speaking skills through the contents of the *Reader*. In the evenings, in their upstairs rooms over Kimball's, Mary and Laura performed their pieces and practiced such selections as *"The Polish Boy," "The Burial of Sir John Moore," "The High Tide," "The Pied Piper," "Tubal Cain," "Paul Revere's Ride," and "The Village Blacksmith."* Men in the store below liked to gather silently to listen to the Ingalls girls recite. Laura and Mary had learned the rules of enunciation, articulation, accent, emphasis, inflection, pitch, pause and slur.

Sarah Donlan and William Reed, teachers at the Burr Oak School when Laura attended there.

Laura excelled in reading and spelling, but she admitted that arithmetic was a temporary difficulty during the term at the Burr Oak school. "My greatest problem that spring was that I couldn't get past the multiplication tables at school. I just couldn't memorize it and we couldn't go on in the arithmetic until we could say the multiplication table. Those who passed were going upstairs and I would have to stay behind."

Laura had time to study when Ma asked her to stay home from school and help her when spring approached. Between chores and housework, Laura worked multiplication sums. She reviewed when she needed to, "looking back at the table to help me when I couldn't remember. One day, I suddenly knew all the tables without looking back!"

Pa and Ma decided to move again when a shocking event occurred in the saloon next to Kimball's Grocery, and then right below them in the store. First, Hairpin, Amy's beau, died in the

16

The brick school in Burr oak, where the Ingalls girls attended

saloon. As Laura explained it, he "had been laying dead drunk for several days, came to, and took another drink to sober up. Before he had got it well swallowed, he put a cigar in his mouth and lit it. The flame of the match set fire to the whiskey fumes, he breathed fire into his lungs and died in a few minutes."

As if this were not enough, the grocer and his wife, who lived in the rooms below the Ingalls, woke Pa with their fighting and screaming. Pa went downstairs and "found the grocer crazy drunk... holding a lighted lamp, bottom side up. The kerosene was running out of the lamp and blazing around his hand. Pa made him stop, put him to bed...saying it was a mercy we had not all been burned to death in our sleep."

Mr. Bisbee owned a red-brick house on the outskirts of Burr Oak, where the woods and stone quarry bordered the village. Pa rented it, and the family was settled there by May. His feedmill closed for the season, and Pa knew he would be away from home doing day labor, so he wanted a safe and peaceful home for his girls. "It was a wonderful place to live," Laura recalled. "We were very happy there."

On May 23, 1877, a new baby was born in the brick house. She was another girl, Pa and Ma's last child. They named her Grace Pearl.

Mary and Laura and Carrie all helped Ma care for Grace that summer in the brick house, and were busy with the garden and work inside. Pa bought a cow, and it was Laura's happy chore to take her to the pasture in the morning and bring her home at

17

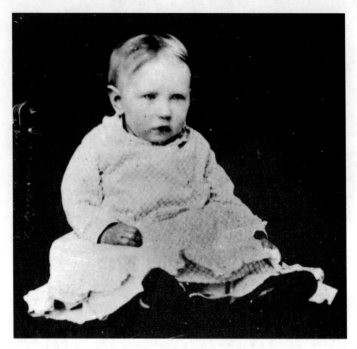

Grace, Pa & Ma's Burr Oak baby.

sunset. "Going after the cow was the happiest time of the day," Laura declared.

When there was time, Laura also wandered in the oak woods, or went walking with Mary and Carrie, Sometimes, she and her school-friend Alice Ward walked the length of Burr Oak to the edge of town and explored the graveyard.

Laura and Alice had to pass the Symmes house on the way to the cemetery. It was a pretty place, covered with ivy and surrounded by roses. But "a boy lived there who was an idiot," Laura said. "Sometimes he came out and acted so strangely...Then an old woman, his grandmother, would beckon us in and offer cookies and roses. But we did not like her, either, and always hurried by."

In the Burr Oak cemetery, Laura enjoyed the flowers and evergreens, the soft grass and moss and the "white stones standing amid all this beauty." She read the names and verses about Burr Oak people who had lived and died before she came to town, and decided this was a very pleasant place to lie and sleep till Judgment Day"

The Burr Oak Cemetery

DARWIN E.
Son of
RICHARD & ADALIZA
SYMMS.
Killed at the battle of
Little Big Horn, with
Custer, June 25, 1876
AGED
25 Yrs. 9 Mos. & 28 Days.

A gravestone which Laura saw in the Burr Oak Cemetery.

That summer of 1877 was busy and interesting for Laura, but Pa and Ma worried about the future. Burr Oak was not their ideal of a home in the West. People knew and liked the Ingalls family, and were aware that their finances were meager. One day when Laura returned with the cow, she found Mrs. Starr, the doctor's wife, visiting with Ma. When Laura came in, Mrs. Starr hugged her close, and explained that her girls Ida and Fanny were away teaching and she was lonesome. The Starrs wanted Laura to live with them. They wanted to adopt her.

Charles Ingalls

The Starrs offered Laura pretty clothes, music lessons and education. They wanted to leave Laura a share of the property when they died, just as they would their own girls.

Laura was shocked at the offer, but Ma just smiled her kind smile. Laura remembered with relief that "Ma thanked Mrs. Starr, but said that she and Pa couldn't possibly spare me."

Not everyone in Burr Oak was as generous with regard to the Ingalls family. Mr. Bisbee wanted his rent money promptly, and sometimes Pa's wages were short. Besides, Pa longed to return to the West. His fiddle played marching. moving songs

Caroline Quiner Ingalls

in the evenings, like *"My Old Kentucky Home," "Swanee River"* and *"There is a Happy Land, Far, Far Away."* Laura was not surprised to learn that her family was going west again.

Pa's problem was paying the doctor bill, the grocery bill, the rent, and buying the needed supplies for the trip back to Walnut Grove.

20

Pa became angry; he offered to send the rent money when they were settled in Walnut Grove again, but Mr. Bisbee threatened to have the law take Pa's team of horses. "No man could say that Pa had ever cheated him out of one red cent." Laura said. But the law was on Mr. Bisbee's side, and they were forced to stay in Burr Oak.

Pa grew more impatient. He said old skinflint Bisbee wouldn't keep him there, law or no law. So, Pa sold the cow to the farmer he worked for, and late one night the girls were awakened to find the house empty and the loaded wagon waiting. They were leaving.

Through the dark, the Ingalls family drove away. Pa was still annoyed. "I never thought," he said, "that I'd be leaving any place between two days." He said he had half a notion to get even with Bisbee by not sending him a cent. But Ma just said, "Now, Charles."

By daybreak, the Ingalls family had crossed the Minnesota state line. After breakfast, they turned west, headed back to western Minnesota, where they knew they would be welcomed in Walnut Grove.

Through the cool autumn air of 1877, Laura reflected on the year in Burr Oak as the wagon rolled west again to Walnut Grove. They had lost Freddie, but gained Baby Grace. They had lived in many places, among many people. Pa had learned that living in an old, crowded place was not for him. And Laura knew, too, that she preferred traveling west and living in the west.

The year in Burr Oak was a short interval in Laura's girlhood as a pioneer girl going west. From Burr Oak, she returned to Walnut Grove to live from 1877-1879. And then she made her last move with her family west to Dakota Territory in 1879. There, in the town of DeSmet, the pioneer girl became a prairie woman, all the time storing up the experiences that would surface years later in her *"Little House"* books.

V. A VISIT FROM ROSE,
A LETTER FROM LAURA

I n the fall of 1932, Rose Wilder Lane was on the verge of attaining perhaps her greatest fame, as the author of *Let the Hurricane Roar.* She had lived on her parents' Rocky Ridge Farm in Mansfield, Missouri since 1928 after she returned to America from a sojourn in Albania. On Rocky Ridge, she added to her literary accomplishments by writing a number of Ozark stories and several books; in 1932, she started writing fiction based on the pioneer period of the mid-west.

Rose embarked on a long automobile trip in September of 1932, with New York City as her ultimate destination. There she planned to convene with her many eastern friends and consult with her literary agent George Bye, about the upcoming book publication *Let the Hurricane Roar.* The business and pleasure trip resulted in Rose's visiting her mother's girlhood home in Burr Oak and her father's boyhood homes in Spring Valley, Minnesota and Malone, New York.

Since Rose disliked driving intensely by the time of the 1932 trip, she was accompanied by her Mansfield friend Corrine Murray. As she always did on trips, Rose kept notebooks handy to record highlights of the journey and details and anecdotes which potentially could find their way into her fiction. When the women stopped in Hannibal, Missouri, Rose noted:

. . . simply an exploiting of Mark Twain--the waitress who said Have you ever read the story of Mark Twain? Which story? Why--the story--when you know he discovered the cave & was lost in it. . .the former cigar-shopkeeper, who is now custodian of the Mark Twain house, [has a statue of a] truly remarkable Arab Negro in the tall brown hat, playing the banjo. Pride of the former cigarshopkeeper, who used to have it in his cigar shop and now keeps it in Mark Twain's house dining room.

Rose may have been disgusted at the lack of knowledge and taste in commemorating Mark Twain in Hannibal, but she recorded in her trip notebook a delight in the countryside as she and Corrine drove north through Iowa. . .

Northern Missouri & south & central Iowa (eastern) have such large, imposing old-fashioned farm-houses— "mansions" they would have been in Mansfield. Iowa rolling land: osage orange hedges, tall old windbreaks growing around the great houses. Large barns. many farm-

steads look almost like a small village. Twelve cars seen in more than 2 hours on beautiful concrete roads, Taylor, Iowa to Keokuk. Iowa City, charming city built around the University, truly imposing & beautiful University buildings, & city goes almost immediately into parks along the Iowa River. One genuinely feels taste, the "center of learning" feeling--5,000 students about, registered. Strangely

Rose Wilder Lane

Italianate impression. Many dark or wavy black Italian heads of hair. Iowa type seems to be fine, sensitive, thin-nosed & thin cheeked, but with a kind of pale fire. Young fellow at filling station thinks depression is good for us; of course it caused much suffering, "but that's all life is anyway" said in passing but with simplicity: not a youthful pessimist pose at all . . .

Rose noted that "Cedar Rapids is beautiful in the European sense", and three years later, when her autobiography was published in the *Saturday Evening Post's* "Who's Who and Why" feature, Rose listed Iowa City and Cedar Rapids as "favorite" cities.

As she traveled north, Rose started asking about an obscure little town: Burr Oak. She was determined to find the red-brick town she had heard about from her mother, the place she had read about in the *Pioneer Girl* manuscript. No one seemed to know anything about an Iowa town by that name.

Years later, Rose described her search to Eileen Charbo, the Kansas historian who did extensive research on the site of *Little House on the Prairie*. . .

Some thirty years ago, driving in Iowa, I thought of seeing Burr Oak, and inquired about it from several sources--postoffices mainly; all assured me that there was no such town as Burr Oak in Iowa. I almost drove through it without noticing it; a little town on the Iowa-Minnesota; border; BURR OAK is written over the entrance to the postoffice on Main Street. It has not changed since my mother was a little girl there. Pa "kept hotel"; the building *is now a residence, the housewife generously showed it to me and gave me a platter once belonging to the hotel, my mother recognized it. A drunken suitor once chased the hotel's cook and fired at her, making a bullet hole in the diningroom door; the hole was still there and the woman living in the house was enchanted by the tale when I told it to her* . . .*

Rose was so enthused with what she found in Burr Oak, that she immediately wrote a postcard to her mother. Laura received this message from her daughter:

Burr Oak   *September 27, 1932*
The pines are still in the cemetery and the hotel building is the same, and I have met an old acquaintance of Mr. Bisbee's who remembers the famous fire and Grandpa Ingalls and Bill Masters who owned the hotel. Everything fine. Concrete highway straight through Burr Oak.

Love,
Rose

Rose did not overlook Burr Oak as a setting for one of her popular short stories. Just as she wove many family names, places and incidents into her novels and short fiction, Rose drew upon her mother's girlhood home when she wrote "Silk Dress" for the *Ladies' Home Journal's* August 1937 issue. The story dealt with a young bride, Sally Garland, who heroically battled with difficulties of farming in the west when her husband left in a weakened condition following an injury. But before John and Sally homesteaded in the west, their home was Burr Oak. This is Rose's beginning of "Silk Dress". . .

They were married at dawn in the old church at Burr Oak, Iowa. The March morning was raw, but everyone in Burr Oak was there. The choir sang, thinly without Sally's contralto, and when the minister asked, "Who gives this woman to be married to this man?" Sally's father answered huskily, " I do."

Her mother was crying. There were prosperous young men in Burr Oak whom Sally might have married. She might have lived in a nice brick house, and joined the Married Ladies' Sodality.

"I, Sarah Jane Goode," she repeated the words, "take

*Letter from Rose Wilder Lane to Eileen Charbo, July 11, 1963. Mrs. Charbo is coincidentally the granddaughter of the proprietor of The American House, the rival hotel to the Masters establishment in Burr Oak.

this man, John Howard Garland, to be my wedded husband, to love, honor and obey, for better or worse, for richer or poorer, in sickness and in health, and forsaking all others I will cleave only unto him, for so long as we both shall live. So help me God."

The wagon was already packed with pots and pans, seeds, tools, carpetbags and well-filled food box. The bed was made up, on bedsprings behind the wagon seat. On it were Sally's quilts and comforters, the Friendship Quilt the girls had given her and the goose-feather pillows. John's buffalo robe was spread over all.

The minister filled out and signed the wedding certificate in their new family Bible. Then Sally changed her dress. She put on a dark green merino and her black cloak. A silken cord around her neck held a small astrakhan-cloth muff which matched her pillbox cap. In the mirror her eyes were large and strange, and she pinched her cheeks to bring back some color.

"Well, you would have your own way, Sally," her mother said. "So make the most of it. Remember it's your duty to obey your husband, and try not to act too headstrong against him. Oh, Sally, I'm going to miss my girl!"

Her father said, "You got a good man, Sally; be a good wife to him; God bless you!"

John wiped the wagon wheel clean. he helped her to climb up and tucked the lap rope around her. They said good-by to all the crowding faces; she could not see them very well, but she kept on smiling. The horses settled into their collars and the wagon began to move. Burr Oak was left behind. The horses turned westward and went on steadily. Grass was green along the roadside, and the bare trees were knobby with buds. The wind blew the horses' manes and tails. Such wind, with the sunshine, would soon dry the fields . . .

As a skilled creative writer, Rose often used settings, character composites and life experiences which she wove into the anonymous fabric of fiction. But she was sometimes surprised when her readers assumed that she was using facts and situations which they recognized. "Silk Dress" elicited mail from "Gentle Readers" (as Rose called them), inquiring about Rose's own connection with Burr Oak. When Rose explained that she had not lived in Burr Oak, but that her mother had, it was discovered that one of the letter writers was an old school-mate of Laura's, named Mary Landon.

Laura was delighted when Rose forwarded the letters from old Burr Oakers. "I enjoyed the letters from your G.R.'s [Gentle Readers] very much and shall write to them at once," Laura told Rose. "Strange," she mused, "how the old timers would all like to go back to those old, hard times. They had something that seems to be lost. Perhaps it is our youth."

Laura also told Rose about remembering Mary Landon:

Mary Landon was an utterly strange name to me. It didn't bring an echo of Burr Oak. But just as I began to go to sleep that night, I saw, in my mind, the old school house. Two stories high it was. At the back a woodshed had been built against it over the windows on that side. The peak of the slant roof of the woodshed came up under the eaves of the school building and the joists where the ceiling of the shed should have been, reached from its far side to about two feet below the second story window of the school house and were fastened there against its wall.

We could raise the windows and step out and down into an end of a joist timber. The wood was in one corner of the shed below and looked like a small pile. The rest of the way there was nothing below the joist but the ground ten feet or so below us.

No one thought we would do such a thing, but at noon when both teachers were gone, we used to raise the windows, climb out onto the joists and run across and back, seeing who would go our farthest and run back quickest.

*I saw it, I said, as I was going to sleep and out in the middle of the joist stood a slim, black-haired girl who flapped her arms against her sides like wings and **crowed** to beat any rooster. Mary Landon! Will I write to her! Manly came into the bedroom to see what I was laughing about.*

I was so surprised that she said I was good looking. I always thought I was the homeliest girl ever and the only way I could endure myself was because I could outdo the boys at their games and forget I wasn't pretty. Funny!

I have enjoyed the letters.

Rose's story and the resulting correspondence which she and Laura shared with a few Burr Oakers solidified a tenuous knowledge that the Ingalls family was once connected with the Iowa town. By the time Laura finished her writing of the "Little House" series in 1943, the books were well-known in the midwest. Rumors persisted that Laura once lived in Burr Oak, so finally the editor of the *Decorah Public Opinion* wrote Rose asking for substantiation. The editor, L. Dale Ahern, received a reply from Rose, who referred him to her mother. Laura was pleased to learn of the interest when she opened this letter from Editor Ahern:

Mrs. A. J. Wilder   *May 28, 1947*
Rocky Ridge Farm
Mansfield, Mo.

Dear Mrs. Wilder:

I have a letter from your daughter, Rose Wilder Lane, in which she tells me that you lived in Burr Oak (Winneshiek County) for a year or two in the early 1870's. I am especially interested in this, since my readers often speak to me of your having lived in the Burr Oak community.

Since your daughter informs me that you have "very clear memories of the place and people" who lived around Burr Oak at the time you were there, I should like very much to have you write to me briefly of your recollections of Burr Oak. Anything that you wish to contribute on this subject will be very welcome.

There are people living around Burr Oak now who say they remember you pleasantly, and I can assure you they would be very happy to have an opportunity to read what you might have to say regarding your reminiscences of the community.

Yours sincerely,

L. Dale Ahern

Laura complied with the editor's request. In her usual style of composition, a pen and ink, she drafted the following letter, which was published in the *Public Opinion* on June 18, 1947:

Dear Sir:

My family did live in Burr Oak for nearly two years, but I fear my memories of that time will not be very interesting as they are more of the place than the people.

27

At first we lived in the old Masters hotel. My parents were partners in the business with the new owners, Mr. and Mrs. Steadman.

Their two boys, Jimmy and Reuben, were about the age of my sister Mary and myself and of course we played and quarreled together.

The hotel still stood when Rose saw it a few years ago, as it was then even to the bullet hole in the door between the dining room and kitchen. It was made when the young man of the house, being drunk, shot at his wife who slammed the door between them as she escaped. This had happened some years before, but the bullet hole in the door was thrilling to us children.

Pa used to play his fiddle in the hotel office, and one of the boarders, a Mr. Bisbee, taught me to sing the notes of the musical scale.

We stayed there most of the winter, then moved to rooms over Kimball's grocery.

One night Ma woke Mary and me, telling us to dress quickly. The second building from us, a saloon, was burning and we must be ready to leave quickly if the fire should spread toward us.

Ma and Mary and I stood at the window where we watched the flames and the men in the street carrying buckets of water from the town pump to pour on the fire. Pa was one of them.

The men stood in line. One would fill his bucket and run with it to the fire, while the next man instantly took his place. On returning he took his place at the end of the line, which was constantly moving.

But they all stood still for some moments, with the same man at the pump. At every stroke of the pump handle he would throw up his head and shout "Fire".

Then someone pushed him away and took his place. The bucket into which he was so frantically pumping water had no bottom in it.

The fire was put out after a while and we all went back to bed.

Mary and I were going to school. It seemed to us a big school, but as I remember there were only two rooms. One began in the downstairs room and when advanced enough was promoted upstairs.

Down stairs we learned to sing the multiplication tables to the tune of Yankee Doodle.

Laura and Almanzo Wilder at their Rocky Ridge Farmhouse, 1948.

Next term we went upstairs to the principal, whose name was Reid and who came from Decorah. He was an elecutionist and I have always been grateful to him for the training I was given in reading. I still have the old independent Fifth Reader from which he taught us to give life to "Old Tubal Cain, The Polish Boy and Paul Revere".

We had friends among our school mates. I remember their faces and occassionally the names escape me.

In the spring we moved to a little brick house at the edge of town. It was a happy summer. I loved to go after the cows in the pasture by the creek where the rushes and the blue flags grew and the grass was so fresh and smelled so sweet. I could see the old stone quarry, but was forbidden to go to it as it was filled with water.

Often on Sunday afternoons my friend, Alice Ward, and I would walk out on the other side of town, past the Sims' rose-covered cottage to the graveyard. We would wander in the shade of the great trees, reading the inscriptions on the tomb stones. The grass was green and short and flowers were everywhere. It was a beautiful, peaceful place.

I spent a great deal of time that summer caring for Baby sister, Grace, with the big blue eyes and soft fine hair.

That fall we left Burr Oak and drove in our covered wagon back to Walnut Grove, Minn., and the banks of Plum Creek.

As you see, these are just dim childish memories, but I have thoughts of Burr Oak as a lovely place.

Yours sincerely,
Laura Ingalls Wilder

29

VI. Iowa's Interest in Laura Ingalls Wilder

Immediately after the first "Little House" book appeared in 1932, letters started descending on Laura Ingalls Wilder, praising her work and encouraging her to continue her writing. Because the books had their setting in the mid-west, the impact was unusually great in Wisconsin, Minnesota, Iowa and the Plains States. And since Iowa's pioneer history was similar to the tales described in the "Little House" books, response to Laura's writing was always considerable in the fan mail she received.

After her first two books were published, Laura received this letter from an enthused teacher in Tipton, Iowa:

January 6, 1935

Mrs. Laura Ingalls Wilder
Rocky Ridge Farm
Mansfield, Missouri

My Dear Mrs. Wilder,
We have just finished reading "Farmer Boy" and are just as enthusiastic as we were about "The Little House in the Big Woods."

I am teaching 6th grade now and have the same group of children I had in 4th grade two years ago when we read "Little House in the Big Woods". They were delighted when "Farmer Boy" was published and are hoping for another book written by you.

My pupils are interested in you, personally. They ask dozens of questions--who you live with, what you look like--and so many more. Would it be asking too much of you to answer some of these questions, and maybe a snapshot?

Sincerely yours,
Alfarata Allen Walsh

Children's letters from Iowa were frequently among the stacks of fan mail Laura opened and always answered.

In 1948, she wrote the following letter to Roula Palmer, a young reader from Oelwein, Iowa:*

---

*In 1989, Mrs. Kathryn Fick, who had been Roula Palmer's teacher in Oelwein, visited the museum in Burr Oak and provided the copy of the treasured letter from Laura.

Mansfield Missouri
Nov. 3ᵈ 1948

Dear Roula,

I am glad you and your schoolmates enjoy my books.

The enclosed broucher will tell you about us.

We are not farming now for Almanzo is 92 years old and I am 82, so you see why we can not run a farm any more.

We have one child, Rose Wilder Lane whose home is in Connecticut. You may know of her for she is a writer.

I am the only one of my family living now.

Yours sincerely
Laura Ingalls Wilder

An especially close friendship developed between Laura and an admiring teacher named Ida Carson who first wrote from Glidden, Iowa. Miss Carson used the "Little House" books extensively in her classroom, and periodically wrote to Laura. She enclosed pictures of her students and herself, and Laura's replies indicate that she considered her Iowa correspondent more a personal friend than a fan. Through the years, Laura shared many interesting anecdotes about herself and life on Rocky Ridge Farm. These are some highlights...

In 1946, Laura wrote:

"On our several visits back to DeSmet we came away still unsatisfied. The country and the town are so changed from the old, free days that we seem not able to find there what we were looking for. Perhaps it is our lost youth we were seeking in the place where it used to be..."

"I too sometimes long for the prairies but South Dakota has changed so much it is a disappointment when we go back. I think going back anywhere is apt to disillusion anyone..."

In 1950, after Almanzo's death, Laura wrote to assure Ida Carson of her well-being on Rocky Ridge Farm:

"There are neighbors just across the road and a short distance at the side. Groceries are delivered at the door; mail every morning at the box by the road; my fuel oil tank for my heater is kept filled with no trouble to me and electricity and telephone ready at my touch. The house is warm and comfortable, two boys from the neighbors on the East come every day to see if there is anything they can do for me and a taxi from town is on call to take me wherever I wish to go. Friends from town, only ¼ mile away come often to see me..."

The Sioux City Journal recognized Laura Ingalls Wilder's great contribution as a writer of a pioneer mid-west, but was not aware of her long-ago residence in Iowa. On March 21, 1954, a feature story about Laura and her books was published. Always quietly proud of recognition of her work, Laura pasted the story in her scrap-book.

In Laura's old hometown of Burr Oak, the "Little House" books were introduced to students there through the efforts of a teacher in the village school, Dorothy Emmons. During the years she taught there, 1943-1951, Dorothy could get the "Little House" books from the Winneshiek Circulating Library in Decorah, but she could not always obtain them in sequence for the Burr Oak students to read.

Mrs. Emmons and her pupils produced a program of songs and recitations, followed by a basket lunch sale during one of the school years. With the proceeds, a complete set of "Little House" books was purchased for the Burr Oak school. Thinking that Laura would be interested in the project, Mrs. Emmons wrote her about the children and how interested they were in her stories. They often clamored for a few extra minutes of reading from Laura's books during the daily reading aloud at noon-time. Laura responded with a letter of appreciation.

Burr Oak, years after the Ingalls family was there. The hotel, with an addition, is to the right of the town pump and wind mill.

After retiring from teaching, Dorothy Emmons served as Burr Oak's postmaster from 1956-1975. In that capacity, she periodically met interested readers of the Wilder books who came to Burr Oak seeking some remnant of history concerning Laura's family. Bernice Risse, an Osage, Iowa teacher, came seeking facts; for many years she was assistant curator at the Laura Ingalls Wilder Home and Museum in Mansfield.

In the fall of 1968, Lewis and Irene Lichty arrived in Burr Oak with a special interest in the Ingalls history there. They were among the founders of the Laura Ingalls Wilder Home Association in Mansfield, and served as first curators. Because of constant questioning about the Burr Oak years, the Lichtys were determined to find answers for the many tourists they welcomed at the Wilder Home. They visited with Burr Oak people, walked through the cemetery where Laura had wandered, and uncovered facts about the Ingalls' lives in Iowa. The result was Irene V. Lichty's booklet, *The Ingalls Family From Plum Creek To Walnut Grove Via Burr Oak, Iowa.* It was published in 1970, and served as a welcome source for those who wondered about the missing years between *On The Banks of Plum Creek* and *By The Shores of Silver Lake.*

The Lichtys' visit and the resulting publication stirred renewed interest in the fact that Burr Oak was the former home of a renowned writer. Local citizens felt concerned that the former Masters Hotel was unmarked and in a dilapidated condition. With a steady stream of readers now trailing into Burr Oak, it was evident that a national interest in the town as a literary landmark was a reality. The obvious goal became apparent: the Masters Hotel needed to be restored and opened as a museum.

VII. THE REBIRTH OF THE MASTERS HOTEL

By the early 1970s, the former home of Laura Ingalls Wilder in Burr Oak was falling into ruin. The roof leaked, siding was rotten, foundations were collapsing and power and plumbing were inoperative. The old Burr Oak House, later the Masters Hotel, stood seemingly dejected and forgotten along Burr Oak's quiet Main Street. Few of the one hundred residents of the town regarded it as more than an nuisance.

To outsiders, the old hotel looked fit for demolition. But to four Iowans, the building represented a unique period of Burr Oak past. And they were determined to preserve it. Three educators and a native Burr Oaker were the driving forces for the transformation of an eyesore to a literary landmark.

The four friends with a cause were Lynn Danielson, school librarian; David De Cou of Burr Oak, and teachers Lorraine Houck and Jean Jenkins. Each of them felt excitement as the project started...

Jean Jenkins said that, "I saw the hotel restoration project as a natural step in the progression of making the *"Little House"* series a permanent part of Iowa history. I had first met the books as a fifth grader in a one-room school. Later, as an Iowa teacher, I read them to my fourth, fifth and sixth graders."

Lorraine Houck also loved reading the Wilder books to her students. After she heard of the Lichtys' visit to Burr Oak in 1968, she and her family stopped in Burr Oak to view the hotel. Little did they know that they looked at the wrong one! When Lorraine learned that the actual Masters Hotel was for sale, "I asked my husband what he would say if I signed a note to purchase a falling down hotel, and he said it was OK!"

Lynn Danielson first became aware of Burr Oak as Laura's home when a letter was turned over to him at the North Winneshiek school library, asking for verification of Burr Oak as Laura's onetime home. He began searching for facts, and then was contacted by Jean and Lorraine about the possiblity of restoring the hotel. Lynn said the hotel was "pretty hopeless" when the unofficial committee went to look it over. The owners, Mr. and Mrs. Lawrence Donlan of Cresco, were contacted. Lynn recalled: "I remember that I tried to emphasize to the couple that they would get satisfaction in seeing the old building restored and turned into a museum."

34

David De Cou of Burr Oak had passed the old hotel all his life and grew to appreciate the Wilder books when they were read aloud in his country school. "Then," said David, "what could be better than discovering that Laura had actually lived in the same town as I did! But one day, when some Laura fans were looking at the building across the street from the actual site, I walked over and told them I was sure they were looking at the wrong building!"

As an important detail, before purchasing the old Masters Hotel, the four enthusiasts determined that they were pinpointing the right property. Many assumed that the still-standing American House hotel* was the actual Ingalls home. It had erroneously been pictured in the Lichty book, which many visitors used as a guide in Burr Oak. David De Cou spent time in the courthouse in Decorah searching out old land transactions, and ascertained that the hotel for sale was indeed the right one.

In 1973, the hotel was purchased for $1,500 and turned over to the newly formed non-profit organization called the Laura Ingalls Wilder Park and Museum. The De Cous donated land next to their historic old general store to allow generous grounds to surround the forthcoming museum.

The addition to the old hotel enlarged it considerably in this picture taken around 1920.

The hotel had undergone structural changes in the years after the Ingalls family had lived there. A wing had been added by F.C. Schank during his occupancy. Fortunately, a photograph of the early era of the Burr Oak House in George Bent's book showed the hotel exactly as it had been in the 1870s. The photo was used as a restoration guide.

* The American House was demolished soon after the former Ingalls home was purchased for restoration.

Funds were needed to support the massive needs of transform-
ing a decrepit building into a fitting memorial to a famous writer.
Lorraine Houck organized a "Pennies for Laura" drive, asking for
help from elementary students in Iowa and neighboring states.
The response was amazing. Donations came from many states. A
ten-year old girl in the Burr Oak area even donated two of her
live chickens!

The hotel during restoration, 1975.

Benefit auctions, dinners, dances, bake sales and book sales all
helped gather funds for the hotel restoration. Many local groups
assisted in actual labor needed to renovate the building. The 389ᵗʰ
Engineer Battalion of the Army Reserve stationed in Decorah
worked for ten weekends on the project. Among the
accomplishments were foundation work, electrical wiring, re-
roofing and re-siding, installing new windows, re-building the
stairway, replacing flooring, building a chimney and painting.

The interior of the re-emerging hotel also required much labor.
On the lower floor, the dining room and kitchen were restored.
The door with bullet holes was not found, but old cupboards still
existed which certainly dated back to the Ingalls era.

On the ground floor, the former bar-room was established as a
reception area for tourists and a sales room for books. The hotel
parlor was arranged with period furnishings. The organ which
was donated had special significance, as it was a George Bent
model. The two bedrooms on the ground floor were filled with
clothing of the era, including some apparel of Mr. Reed, Laura's
teacher. Elementary students in Cottage Grove, Oregon pieced
and donated a quilt for one of the beds.

The hotel after restoration

Four upstairs bedrooms were also furnished to appear as they did in the 1870s. Many of the antique furnishings were loaned or donated to the museum. Only a few artifacts were purchased.

The yard behind the restored hotel was not neglected in the overall restoration. A footbridge was built over Silver Creek. The site of the old flowing spring was re-established. The grounds were landscaped and recreational equipment was placed so that children could play where the Ingalls girls and Steadman boys had played. A covered picnic shelter was constructed so that travelers could rest and eat as they had a century before in the hotel.

The foresight and determination of four Laura Ingalls Wilder admirers resulted in the grand opening of the re-created Masters Hotel. A Laura Ingalls Wilder Bi-Centennial Celebration was held on June 4-5-6, 1976. The project, stated David De Cou, "involved the entire community in group effort and was truly a labor of love for a little girl who once lived in Burr Oak."

A Bent organ in the hotel parlor [Joan L. Zug Photo]

In the years since its opening as a museum, the Masters Hotel has continued to preserve the old building and add to its rich collection of artifacts from the pioneer era. Reminding visitors of the stop Rose Wilder Lane made in Burr Oak is a set of ivory birds from her home, a gift of her adopted grandson, Roger Mac Bride.

"Little House" enthusiasts immediately added Burr Oak to treks to the other book sites in Pepin, Wisconsin, Walnut Grove, Minnesota, Independence, Kansas, DeSmet, South Dakota and Mansfield, Missouri. Each year the number of summer visitors increased markedly because of widespread publicity and word-of-mouth. Burr Oak's connection with Laura Ingalls Wilder became increasingly well-known through the 1980s. A television documentary, "Laura Ingalls Wilder: An American Pioneer Girl," was produced in 1985 and brought even more recognition of the Burr Oak site.

When visitors come to Burr Oak seeking roots and remembrances of the Ingalls family, they often search beyond the beautifully restored hotel. Although the character of the quiet little Iowa village is still intact, most of the buildings connected with Laura's stay there are gone.

38

The restored hotel kitchen

Kitchen–Dining room cupboards, probably dating from the Ingalls era.

Mr. Bisbee's bedroom, just off the hotel parlor. [Joan L. Zug Photo]

The brick school attended by the Ingalls girls was replaced by a frame building. The Congregational Church where the Ingalls family worshipped was moved to Main Street around 1905 and converted into a garage and storage shed for machinery. The church bell Laura held was sold to the nearby Hesper Friends Church. The brick house where Grace was born in 1877 was covered with a frame siding and eventually was demolished in the 1970s.

Directly across the street from the Masters Hotel, on a small rise, is a house which Laura remembered well from her Burr Oak days. It belonged to Peter Pfeiffer, a wealthy and prominent Burr Oaker in the 1870s. Laura remembered the owner as "Mr. Pifer," and was much impressed by his home:

Across the street we looked onto a terraced lawn of a big white house. The large house and its grounds filled all of two blocks. Mr. Pifer, who owned this house, was very rich, and the house was beautiful inside as well as out. There were open stairways and marble fireplaces and statues and velvet hangings. But for all this luxury, the house had a stiff, unhomelike air. Mr. Pifer's widowed daughter and her two daughters often came to sit with Ma in our front room [of the rented rooms over Kimball's store], liking it, they said, because it was so bright and cheerful.

Silver Creek still runs behind the restored hotel.

The Burr Oak Cemetery circa 1920

Perhaps the most tangible Ingalls site in Burr Oak, in addition to the hotel, is the cemetery. Quiet and well-kept, it is still a peaceful, pleasant oasis. The weathered grave stones can be easily identified as those seen by Laura by their dates. And, just as they did for Laura, the markers tell stories of long-ago Burr Oak residents. They were not always pleasant histories. The Symmes family stone records the death of son William at the infamous Civil War prison of Andersonville in 1864. In 1876, his brother Darwin was killed with Custer in the Battle of Big Horn.

Burr Oak, Iowa is still a "lovely place" as Laura referred to it. It has taken a unique place in the family of "Little House" sites which are known and loved all over the world.

VIII. IOWA'S OTHER INGALLS ASSOCIATIONS

In her last four "*Little House*" books, Laura never inferred that she had lived in Iowa, but she periodically referred to the state. "Iowa" signified a place of "eastern" styles and a model for trends to be copied and admired by the Ingalls family in their Dakota Territory home. This first is evidenced in *By the Shores of Silver Lake,* when the Ingalls family became acquainted with Robert and Ella Boast from Iowa.

The Boasts arrived from Iowa at Christmas-time, 1879, settling along Silver Lake in Dakota Territory, where the Ingallses were wintering. Laura was immediately enchanted by stylish Mrs. Boast. Through the winter of 1879-1880, she was constantly updating Ma and the girls as to Iowa styles and fads. "She said everyone in Iowa was making whatnots," Laura wrote in *By the Shores of Silver Lake.* When Pa made one for Ma, he declared "And there's nothing too good in Iowa for you, Caroline."

Laura spoke of their Iowa friends, the Boasts, as newlyweds. But they had been married a decade when they arrived to homestead at what became DeSmet, Dakota Territory. They were youthful and cheery company, so perhaps Laura thought of the Boasts as recently wed. They had come from New Hartford, Iowa. Mr. Boast was born in Quebec in 1848, but he met and married Ella Rosina Peck in Iowa.

"Lifelong friends" were the words Carrie used to describe the Boasts and the Ingalls families.

* * *

Much later, another Iowa couple entered the Ingalls family life. They were Ernest and Minnie Green. In 1902, soon after Pa's death, Ma rented rooms in the family home in DeSmet. One of her first roomers was Ernest Green, a lawyer from Ocheyedan, Iowa. His young wife Minnie had no household duties to occupy her, so she often spent her afternoons sitting in the parlor with Mrs. Ingalls and blind Mary. They became very close.

Lawyer Green eventually became legal counsel to Ma and her daughters in their small business matters of wills and property exchanges. Finally, the rental and sale of the Ingalls home in DeSmet was handled by Judge Green.

The three Green children, Blanche, Ralph and Paul, knew Ma as "Grandma Ingalls." They often stopped to visit on their way to school and back, after the Greens had moved to a home of their own. Both Ma's and Mary's funerals were held from the

Ernest and Minnie Green

hospitable Green home in DeSmet.

Laura Ingalls Wilder knew of the care and attention the kindly Iowans gave to her mother and sisters. Finally, in 1931, Laura met Minnie Green. The Wilders were visiting DeSmet, and with Grace, Laura "called on Mrs. Green, who is a very nice person and spoke so sweetly of Ma and Mary." Minnie Green told Laura that "Ma was a mother to her when she first came to DeSmet and lived in the house with her." "I like Mrs. Green, " Laura said.

Ernest Green's sister Freda became aquainted with Ma and Mary on a visit she made to DeSmet immediately following her high school graduation in 1905. The young Iowa girl was immediately introduced to the Ingalls family. "Minnie took her sister and me to visit them, being very fond of the Ingalls family." said Freda. "I went many times afterward. Mrs. Ingalls was sweet and gentle, like my little mother. On one of my visits there was a cord hammock hanging on the wall that Mary had made; she also showed me the cord fly horse nets that she made."

Later, as librarian for over twenty-seven years in Little Rock, Iowa, Freda Green had the pleasure of introducing and buying many copies of the *"Little House"* books by Laura for her patrons. During the 1970s, she was interviewed several times concerning her connection with the Ingalls family. She was happy to provide interesting data on her memories of the Ingalls home in DeSmet during its restoration.

* * *

The state of Iowa became a mecca of educational hope for the Ingalls family following Mary's blindness in 1879. When Pa and Ma heard that there was a college for the blind at Vinton, Iowa, it became their goal to send Mary there. The last four *"Little House"* books chronicle the family's work, preparation, and saving towards Mary's education at Vinton.

The school which was so important to Mary Ingalls was known as the Iowa College for the Blind when it opened at Vinton in 1862. It was still sometimes called the "Asylum for the Blind" and the street in front of the school building known as "Asylum Street." But the school was known for its progressive and modern methods of training its students and the term "asylum" was disdained.

When Mary was sixteen, in the fall of 1881, Pa and Ma took her to Vinton to enroll in the school. Laura recalled that Dakota Territory had no facility for training its blind, but a tuition agreement existed with Iowa for students like Mary. It is unclear what expenses the Ingalls family contributed to Mary's education, but through the *"Little House"* books, we know that they sacrificed for Mary's sake.

IOWA INSTITUTION
FOR THE
EDUCATION OF THE BLIND.

An old engraving shows the Iowa College for the Blind during Mary's era there.

When Pa and Ma got Mary settled in school in November, 1881, they were impressed with the Main Building of the college. According to *Gleanings from our Past*, a history of the Iowa Braille and Sight Saving School, the college facility was outstanding even then:

> *The north and south wings of the school with their long verandas, and the even longer veranda across the back of the building, commanded an outstanding view. A gravel path led from the stone gate to the front porch with its wooden steps. A stone wall between two and three feet high fronted the east edge of the campus. All of these, along with the curving cinder driveway and the many trees and shrubs, helped create the distinctive image.* *

Mary was sixteen when she started school in Vinton; she would continue her Iowa education until she graduated at the age of twenty-four. Those years seem to have been the highlight of her life. Not only did her schooling broaden her many interests and strong intellect, it also gave her a happy sociability with other blind students. When Mary enrolled in 1881, there were 94 other students at Vinton.

Mary of course learned to read and write Braille and she also mastered raised, or embossed print. Eventually she had a small library of those books. Her Braille slate is at the Laura Ingalls Wilder Home and Museum in Mansfield. School books and one volume of her embossed print Bible are on display in DeSmet. Both museums have examples of her beadwork. Mary was also able to learn to write in pencil to seeing friends, using the grooves in her slate as a guide to straight lines.

The curriculum at the Iowa College for the Blind was a rigorous mix of academic and manual training. During the 1884-1885 school year, Mary was classed as a "Second Junior." Her course-work included Music, in which she was graded 65; Arithmetic, 98; U.S. History, 96; History, 98 and Physiology, 99. She also studied Piano, Beadwork, Sewing and Reading that year.

* Gleanings from our Past, 1984, was published by the Iowa Braille and Sight Saving School at Vinton.

In later years at school, Mary's course-work included Natural History, Chemistry, Rhetoric, Algebra, Political Economy and Literature. The subjects were all on a college level. Her musical performance included both piano and organ, and was rated as exceptional. She took courses in "Fancy Work" and mastered beadwork, carpet weaving, sewing, knitting and the making of hammocks and fly nets for horses.

Mary in the 1880's, photographed at Star Gallery, Vinton, Iowa.

A day at the Iowa College for the Blind in Mary's time was governed by bells and fairly rigid organization. The first bell rang at 6:00 for rising, followed by breakfast and Chapel at 7:15. Academic classes were held until the noon dinner. The afternoons were filled with music classes, industrial training and physical training activities. Supper was at 5:30, followed by Chapel at 7:00. A reading period was scheduled until 9:00 bedtime.

Thomas F. McCune became superintendent of the Iowa College for the Blind during Mary's first year there. He was dedicated to both excellence and innovation. One of McCune's theories was that there should be less segregation of the sexes at the school. Boys and girls were allowed to mix during socials, on the playground, and during club and committee work. At meetings of the Literary Society, of which Mary was a member, dancing was encouraged.

Mary was classed as a tenth grader when she left school to return home to DeSmet on April 27, 1887. She spent the next school year, 1887-1888 at home in DeSmet. Records show that she was often in the school infirmary, so it is likely that her health was poor. For many years, she suffered from the after-effects of the "brain fever" (meningitis) which had taken her sight.

During her last year at Vinton, 1888-1889, Mary took reading, writing and literature courses. She had already started writing poetry, and she continued to produce verse for the rest of her life. At the final entertainment of her literary society before graduation, Mary recited "Memory." And at graduation exercises on June 12, 1889, Mary performed the Burns essay, "Bide a Wee and Dinna Weary," for the assembled crowd and her graduating class of eight.

Mary was twenty-four when she finished her education in Iowa. Though she spent the rest of her days living contentedly in little houses in South Dakota, often her mind wandered back to the happy days she had spent at the Iowa College for the Blind.

* * *

The first member of the Ingalls family to achieve wide fame as a writer was Laura's daughter, Rose Wilder Lane. Through her career as a novelist and journalist, Rose was acquainted with many of the world's most prominent artists, authors, politicians and celebrities. Few of her associations pleased her as much as her friendship with Iowa's native son, President Herbert Hoover.

Rose saw in Hoover the greatness she most appreciated: a man born close to the soil, who grew to prominence using integrity, courage and fundamental American convictions. She and Hoover shared the belief that the concept of personal liberty was integral to the development and well-being of each individual. Both of them abhorred the image of an enlarged federal government which infringed on the personal choices and independence of citizens.

Rose Wilder Lane and Herbert Hoover both were born of pioneer stock in the heartland of America. In principle, the influence of Hoover's birthplace at West Branch, Iowa was not unlike Rose's prairie origins at DeSmet, South Dakota. Of Hoover, Rose wrote: "The spirit of five generations of American pioneers was his spirit...their lives had gone to the making of America; his life was to be part of the future."

In 1920, Rose wrote the *Sunset Magazine* serial, "The Making of Herbert Hoover." The book version also appeared the same year. "This is a story stranger than fiction and as real as America. Herbert Hoover represents America," Rose wrote. In her book she chronicled Hoover's life from his Iowa origins to his masterful work in administering food relief in Europe following World War I.

Although she had written the Hoover book at the beginning of her career, it was not until Rose retired from active authorship in the early 1940s that she resumed a close association with the ex-president. When she ceased writing fiction, Rose became intensely interested in exploring and writing about American democracy and personal liberty. These were areas which Rose and Hoover discussed at length.

In 1942, while Rose was preparing her book *Discovery of Freedom,* Hoover read the manuscript. He said. "The basic idea of the book is superb. Its optimism is a tonic to the soul."

48

Hoover firmly believed in Rose's thesis in *Discovery of Freedom:* that all men were inherently free, and should resist any authority or philosophy which threatens personal liberty.

During the 1940's, when Hoover's offices were in the Waldorf-Astoria in New York and Rose's home was in nearby Danbury, Connecticut, the two were in regular communication. Hoover invited Rose to conference with him and others about vital issues, and he complimented her writings extravagantly. He suggested that a mass printing of Rose's *Give Me Liberty* would be greatly helpful in counteracting collectivist influences in America.

"I might bring you one of my real midwestern apple pies," Rose remarked as she and the ex-president planned a lunch meeting together in 1948. That typified the relationship between Herbert Hoover from Iowa, and Rose Wilder Lane, from South Dakota: exchanging pies and principles from thoroughly American roots. "I guess the trouble with you and me is that we belong to some other generation," Hoover wrote Rose.

After their deaths, Hoover's in 1964, and Rose's in 1968, the recorded thoughts and written words of the Iowa president and the mid-western writer were destined to be preserved together. The Herbert Hoover Presidential Library at West Branch, Iowa not only serves as an archive for the thirty-first president's papers, but also for those whose work parallels his administration or philosophy. Because of Rose Wilder Lane's close connection with Hoover as his biographer and political confidant, her adopted grandson and literary heir Roger Mac Bride selected the Hoover Library as a repository for her papers.

In 1980, the Rose Wilder Lane Papers were added to the archives of the Hoover Library at West Branch. They cover many aspects of the Rose's varied and productive life. There are files pertaining to her career as a novelist. Collections of correspondence attest to Rose's staunch support of Americanism. Her life as a traveling correspondent throughout the world is documented by her many diaries and journals. And letters, manuscript fragments and other documentation reveals Rose's input and assistance with her mother's authorship of the *"Little House"* books.

With the flourishing Masters Hotel restoration in Burr Oak, and the rich repository of facts preserved among the Rose Wilder Lane Papers at the Hoover Library in West Branch, Iowa can proudly claim its place in *"Little House"* lore.

I X. I Remember Burr Oak
With Pleasure

Mansfield, Mo,
November 5 & 1951

Dear Mrs Weldon,

  I am pleased that you and
your pupils like my stories and glad indeed
that you love me. The reason the stories
seem so real is because they are true.

  When I was a small child I lived with my
parents and sisters in Burr Oak two years
The reason I did not put it in my stories
was that it would bring in too many
characters. You know in writing a story
the readers interest must be held to the
principal people, not scattered among so
many. I remember Burr Oak with pleasure

  My daughter, Rose Wilder Lane, visited the
town some years ago.

  I am the only one of my family living now,
After sister Mary graduated from college
she lived at home, busy with her books
and music and all the work she had
learned to do so well.

Sisters Carrie and Grace married and left home, Carrie to go to the Black Hills near Mt. Rushmore and Grace to a farm only seven miles from De Smet.

Both they and their husbands died several years ago leaving no children,

Plum Creek is about 2½ miles North of Walnut Grove, Minnesota, I recently had a letter from people who had just visited the place and found the site of our old dugout on the bank.

Silver Lake was ½ mi East of De Smet. It has been drained so there is no lake there now. It was a small lake, fed by springs that were destroyed in the draining,

I have so many letters and callers that I can not remember any individuals. My memory is not what it used to be,

With love to you and your pupils,

Yours sincerely
Laura Ingalls Wilder

X.   Welcome to Burr Oak

When Rose Wilder Lane visited Burr Oak in 1932, she may well have inquired at the Burr Oak Savings Bank in her search for the hotel where her mother once lived. The brick building, which was established in 1910, was on it last legs when Rose came to town, but it stood across the street from the hotel Rose sought. A year earlier two men robbed the brick bank. Employees were herded into the bank vault while the criminals made their getaway. Two weeks later they were apprehended in Indiana, and both were sentenced to life in prison. The bank continued to operate until 1933.

If Rose heard that story, chances are she might have incorporated some of the details in one of her popular magazine short stories written in the 1930s. But her search was for a gentler past in Burr Oak, when the wooden hotel building across the street sheltered the Ingalls family.

After the Burr Oak Savings Bank closed , the tidy little building had another life as a barber shop, and later as a post office. Then, with Burr Oak's population dwindling, the building fell into disrepair.   In 1999 the property was purchased by the Laura Ingalls Wilder Park and Museum. It merited a listing on the National Registry of Historic Places.

Because administrative space and an orientation place was lacking in the hotel museum, the bank building, just a few steps away, was seen as an ideal place to welcome the visitors to Burr Oak's Laura Ingalls Wilder site. Then acting director, Ferneva Brimacomb wrote many grants and headed up fundraising efforts to restore the bank building. It was transformed into a fine reception place for visitors in the 21st century. Office space, a book and gift shop, and needed storage for the museum evolved as the building was restored.

Laura Ingalls Wilder never saw the former Burr Oak bank, but we can't help but believe she would be happy at the progress made in her girlhood hometown in Iowa.

Travels of the Ingalls Family

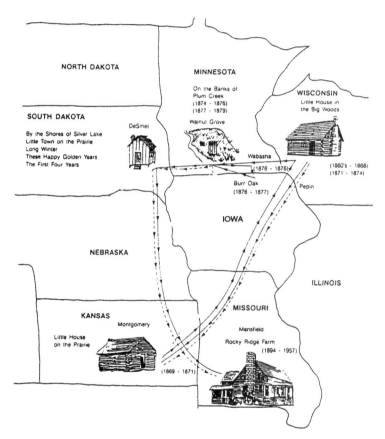

From her birthplace in Wisconsin to her final home in Missouri, Laura Ingalls Wilder's pioneering journeys with her family are traced.

Laura Ingalls Wilder Family Series

by

William Anderson

The Story of the Ingalls

The Story of the Wilders

Laura Wilder of Mansfield

A Wilder in the West

Laura's Rose:
The Story of Rose Wilder Lane

The Horn Book's Laura Ingalls Wilder

The Iowa Story of Laura Ingalls Wilder

The Walnut Grove Story of Laura Ingalls Wilder

About the author

William Anderson has written or edited over twenty books. Among his Harper Collins titles are: Laura Ingalls Wilder Country, A Little House Sampler, *and* Laura Ingalls Wilder: A Biography.

Visit him on the web at www.williamandersonbooks.com